THE COUPLE'S
TAO TE CHING

■

ALSO BY WILLIAM MARTIN

The Parent's Tao Te Ching

THE COUPLE'S TAO TE CHING

A NEW INTERPRETATION

ANCIENT ADVICE
FOR
MODERN LOVERS

BY WILLIAM MARTIN

FOREWORD BY HUGH AND GAYLE PRATHER
ILLUSTRATIONS BY HANK TUSINSKI

MARLOWE & COMPANY
NEW YORK

Published by
Marlowe & Company
An Imprint of Avalon Publishing Group Incorporated
245 West 17th Street, 11th Floor
New York, NY 10011

Library of Congress Cataloging-in-Publication Data
Martin, William, 1944–
    The couple's Tao te ching: a new interpretation—
ancient advice for modern lovers / by William Martin.
        p.   cm.
    ISBN 1-56924-650-5
    1. Man-woman relationships.   2. Marriage.
3. Married people.   4. Love.   5. Taoism.   6. Lao-tzu.
Tao te ching.
HQ801.M413   2000
306.7 21—dc21   99-045386

DESIGN BY PAULINE NEUWIRTH, NEUWIRTH & ASSOCIATES, INC.
Printed in the United States of America
Distributed by Publishers Group West

10   9   8   7   6   5

To my own Beloved, Nancy

CONTENTS

■

 I AM FIRST of all grateful to Lao Tzu. Legendary or real, the "Old Boy" has left humanity a transformative manuscript in his brief Tao Te Ching. His marvelous glimpse into the wonders of "the way things work" has been an inspiring guide for two decades of my life.

Matthew Lore, my editor at Marlowe and Company, has been an inspiration as well. His skill at grasping the essence of communication has clarified, tightened, and greatly blessed my work. He has an eye for all the details of production and design that make a book beautiful inside and out.

My agent, Barbara Moulton of San Francisco, has been a friend, encourager, and tireless worker on my behalf. In the midst of helping me give birth to my books, she gave birth to a wonderful daughter and still managed to give me everything an author could ask, and more.

My beloved spouse, Nancy, is hidden and not so hidden in every page of this book. Her gracious love, her wondrous soul, and her lovely eyes have given me windows into the Mystery that has filled my life with light.

All of the people who have expressed to me their appreciation of my previous book, *The Parent's Tao Te Ching*, have encouraged me and blessed me. I am pleased that they found my words helpful. May all lovers who read this book find it helpful as well.

To all of you, my gratitude. Thank you.

■

BRUSH PAINTING IS one of the many practices used to awaken one's participation in and manifestation of the Tao. By focusing and directing the painter's awareness, it is an expedient way to uncover and clarify a painter's state of mind. A brush painter selects a subject, studies it to determine a minimum number of strokes, then orders and repeats these strokes until they become one single, fluid movement, generally executed on one exhalation. The extent to which the practitioner is focused, at one with the materials and techniques, is the extent to which the resulting work is infused with life and vitality of its own.

—*Hank Tusinski*

81 WAYS TO DIVE

FOR MANY YEARS, we have studied great-love relationships. *The Couple's Tao Te Ching* powerfully presents a truth that we also have noticed: Couples who reach the second honeymoon stage—the one that doesn't go away—are not splendid human beings. Nor do they somehow possess great powers or talents. The difference, perhaps the sole difference, is that these couples have finally grown to accept each other deeply. They see one another clearly and no longer *feel the need* to pressure each other to change.

This open-eyed acceptance works the same miracle in relationship after relationship—the shortcomings and imperfections of your partner become part of what you love about this person. Obviously, such transformation is not possible when one or both partners is deeply disturbed and acts destructively toward the other. But if hurtfulness and damage are at the core of a relationship, there *is* no relationship—because the actual relationship has never been experienced. This is why Bill Martin's work is valuable even to couples with profound, chronic issues. Seldom can a relationship book be applied to all stages of a couples' growth, but *The Couple's Tao Te Ching*, being rich in spiritual truth, is a text that can be. Whether opened for quick inspiration or studied for long-term gains, its mystical and poetic nature make it more a living advisor than a book of rigid concepts. Like a loving friend, it gently draws forth our spiritual perception.

Many couples simply are not aware of the oneness that lies quietly in their hearts. As a first step, they must see what they have chosen in its place. This is not necessarily fun. As Bill puts it, "Rather than finding better ways to fight, might you be able to find the roots of your conflicts? This is certainly a difficult task, filled with emotion and fear. But if your goal is discovery instead of defense, deep peace is just ahead."

Mastering techniques on how to manipulate your partner—which is what most relationship books offer—will get you long-term war. Deep awareness of each other and yourself leads to peace. But as Bill points out, looking at yourself and listening to your partner's insights is not always pleasant. Many couples avoid this process, to the doom of their relationship.

You have great insight into your partner. During

an argument, you know exactly what to say to make this person furious, depressed, embarrassed, or scared. So the problem is not insight. The problem is how you habitually *use* insight. Times of honest looking are not times to trade grudges or criticize what you don't like. They are not even times to shame yourself and accept guilt. They are periods of love and tenderness—because you are picking the thorns from each other's feet. And although this isn't palatable, it sure beats the alternative.

Once the process of helping each other is learned, you are ready for what *The Couple's Tao Te Ching* has for you next. Open it up—and no matter what the page—you have an *experience*. The experience touches your heart. And soon your relationship is more relaxed, more enjoyable.

This approach is more natural than trying to understand someone's version of "the five steps" or "the ten rules"; then trying to execute the rules correctly; then trying to analyze and judge the results. Bill is saying we simply don't *need* to go to the Home Depot relationship aisle to fix what we think is wrong. All we need is to dive into the shimmering lake of our relationship. He even gives us 81 ways to dive!

Lao Tzu taught that the truth is true and the truth is now. Bill shows how this applies to our partnerships and marriages. Relationship already exists—even if you just set eyes on the person for the first time, it already exists. It doesn't have to be pieced together, because it's part of what is natural, real, and always present. Your connection with another person is in your heart, and "getting the relationship you want" is not something you ever need worry about. In fact, it isn't even relevant.

Relationship is more like a bud that contains within it an entire blossom than like a box of assorted parts with no manual. We feed and water the roots and stem that hold the bud high. We protect it against the elements. We keep the ground from which it grows well weeded. Yet as the bud begins to unfold, we want nothing more than to enjoy it. We watch in hushed acceptance as each new stage of beauty is revealed—always nourishing, always protecting, always weeding—but never pushing at the petals to go the direction we think best or squeezing the bud to unfold more quickly.

This approach is so fundamental to happy, healthy relationships that we recommend you do as we ourselves are doing: keep this book near, and drink from it often.

—Hugh and Gayle Prather
Parents, ministers, and authors of
Spiritual Parenting, I Will Never Leave You,
and *Spiritual Notes to Myself*
Fall 1999

THE LONGER I work with the Tao Te Ching the more I become convinced that its gentle wisdom and penetrating insight may be applied to all arenas of modern life. Written in the Sixth Century B.C.E., and directed to cultural and political leaders, this series of 81 brief poetic meditations has become the most published book in the world, next to the Bible. It has appeared in countless versions and translations and its themes have been the subjects of countless other books. It is a book of practical observations of the way the natural world seems to work. The word, "Tao" may be translated as "The Way," or, "The Way of Life." I sometimes like to think of it as "The Way Things Naturally Work."

It has been my companion as I have taken the most important journeys of my life: being a parent to my children and being a lover to my spouse. Its great themes of flexibility, patience, compassion, simplicity, and natural virtue have informed all areas of my life. I wrote of these themes and their influence on the parent-child relationship in my earlier book, *The Parent's Tao Te Ching*. I wrote this book, *The Couple's Tao Te Ching*, for any two people in a committed love relationship. I have attempted first to digest each of the 81 chapters of the *Tao Te Ching*; then to express the essence of each as it applies to a couple; and finally to add a few lines of practical advice for consideration.

The love relationship between two people can be the most rewarding and enlightening adventure possible. It can also be the most painful and disappointing of all experiences. The difference between these two extremes can sometimes be a subtle shift in understanding and perception. The ability to love and be loved in natural and satisfying ways lies within each of us. But modern society has overlaid this natural ability with layer upon layer of rules, expectations, and myths until our relationships have become merely one more of the myriad things we have to "do right" in our complex lives. The natural and gentle principles revealed in the *Tao Te Ching* have become lost in the fog. I believe the recovery of these principles is of utmost importance for lovers in our world.

I cannot write words about love without acknowledging my own Beloved Nancy. She is my dear spouse and my soul's mate. She has looked into my soul and discovered there the wonder and beauty I have attempted to avoid and deny. She has revealed to me the essence of the Tao and the mystery of her person. I know the themes of this book are true because I have discovered them in the wonder of our love together. We are not unique. It is worth reiterating: The ability to love each other in natural and fulfilling ways is written into the very nature of each person on earth. I hope that this book will contribute in some small way to the rediscovery of that ability within you. My blessings to you and to your beloved.

Bill Martin
Summer 1999
Chico, California

THE COUPLE'S
TAO TE CHING

■

1

A PASSION
NOT TAMED BY WORDS

Spinning words together to create vows
will not unite two souls.
Pouring over words in marriage manuals
will not pour spirit into a relationship.
Words may speak of love
but they cannot create it.

The union of one soul with another
is born of a passion that must not be tamed by
     words.
Let your words be tools of this passion,
not barriers to it.

Words emerging from love's furnace
will be few but powerful.
A few words of understanding
may heal a wounded heart.
A few words of wisdom
may comfort a lonely soul.
A few words of sensuous longing
may kindle love's embraces.

☯

If you could speak but fifty words
each day to your beloved,
only that and no more,
what would be your words today?

2

THE HEAVEN
OF THE MOMENT

Always thinking of what you like
and what you don't like
exhausts the energy that could be used
to fuel your passion.

Events of life are always changing.
Everything is made new in your life
between the time you read this line . . .
and this one.
Difficult times and joyous times
can follow each other as swiftly.
When good times arrive welcome them.
When they seem to pass, let them go.
When pain arrives do not despair.
It will pass as well.
You will sometimes feel strong and whole,
and sometimes weak and partial.
This is not a problem.
Do not let these things distract you.

☯

When this evening comes,
lie down in each other's arms.
Let the day slip away.
And enjoy the heaven of the moment.

3

DISTRACTIONS

Possessions may burden a relationship.
They distract, delude, and divide
instead of creating closeness and intimacy.
They create confusion and dissatisfaction
instead of peace and joy.

Quiet your noisy mind.
Simplify your busy life.
Reduce your many distractions
so that you and your beloved
might live in deepest joy.

Consider the things you have accumulated.
Do they enhance your love
and increase your intimacy?
Or have they siphoned energy
from the things you once knew to be important;
walks, talks, leisurely love-making, laughter, and
    play?

4

See Clearly

Your love is a great mystery.
It is like an eternal lake
whose waters are always still and clear like glass.
Looking into it you can see
the truth about your life.

It is like a deep well
whose waters are cool and pure.
Drinking from it you can be reborn.

You do not have to stir the waters
or dig the well.
Merely see yourself clearly
and drink deeply.

You don't need,
"Ten Tidy Tips to Tantalize Your Mate."
You need to look deeply into each other's eyes
for fifteen minutes,
no less.
Hold hands.
Breathe deeply.
No talking.
Don't be afraid.
What do you see?

5

WELCOME EACH OTHER

Love dances through the cosmos,
binding together all that is.
Every living thing is welcomed
with never a word of criticism.

Welcome each other
with the same expansiveness.
What pleases you
and does not please you
is of no importance.
Welcome is all that matters.

Can you merely notice the things you like or
    dislike,
without attaching importance to them
or altering the nature of your openness and
    acceptance?
What will be your first words
when next you meet your beloved?
Will they speak of spacious welcoming?

6

BE LIKE MIDWIVES

Your relationship is constantly giving birth
to new wonders in your soul.
It brings forth
dreams and gifts and children,
plans and hopes and accomplishments,
poems and songs and dances,
work and play and rest.
Be like midwives to each other,
bringing comfort and encouragement
to each other's labor.

☯

What is your beloved birthing?
What are you birthing?
What is your relationship birthing?
What sort of prenatal care is needed?
What are the labor pains like?
Are there newborn fruits of your love?
What care do they need?
How can you help?

7

AS FREE AS THE TAO

You are free to be yourself
in the presence of the Tao.
The Tao has no need for a particular response
     from you
and is therefore free to be one with you.
You can be exactly as you are
in the presence of your beloved
for the love between you is free
of judgment and fear.
You do not cling to opinions or judgments.
You are each without agenda.
You are therefore as free as the Tao.

☯

Can you speak to each other of daily life
without fear of criticism?
Criticism is the cancer of relationships.
It feeds on healthy love
and turns it to self-absorption.
Find it early
and cut it out!

8

BE TO EACH OTHER
LIKE WATER

Be to each other like water.
It brings nourishment to all it touches
without effort or strain.
It seeks out the low places
and does not strive to raise itself
above all others.
Do not seek to lord it over your beloved.
There is no hierarchy in a union of souls.
Each of you must flow like a stream
and surround the other with nurture and
     refreshment.

☯

Is there a sense of flow to your life together,
or is there a sense of strain and effort?
Are you competing instead of nourishing?
How will you nourish your beloved today?

9

NOTHING ELSE
WOULD MATTER

The busier you are with important things
the further from each other you will be.
The more you work,
the lonelier you will become.
The more you try to please people,
the more you will become their prisoner.
How much money is enough?
How many purchases are necessary
to secure your happiness?

Enjoy your work,
then forget it.
Let the eyes and arms
of your beloved
wash it all away.

There was a time when you knew,
beyond doubt,
that if you could just wake up
next to this person
every morning,
nothing else would matter.
Remember?

10

WORRY CREATES WALLS

Keep your thoughts from wandering
to worries, frets, and fears.
This only makes your body rigid and tight,
unavailable to your beloved.
Seeing the world through your fears
creates walls.
Seeing the world through your love
creates intimacy.

When I am worried and fretful
I protect myself by withdrawing.
I retreat into my fearful thoughts
as if by imagining the worst
I somehow prepare for it.
Everyone is left outside,
including my beloved,
waiting for me to regain my senses.

11

THE EMPTY SPACE WITHIN

It is the center of the wheel
where the spokes meet
that enables the wheel to move.
Keep yourselves together at the center
and your relationship will roll smoothly.

It is the empty space within
that makes a bowl useful.
Empty yourselves of agendas for each other
and love will fill your relationship.

It is the space within the walls of a house
that gives a family room to live.
Create a space for each other
free from "oughts" and "shoulds"
where you both can safely live,
and all manner of joy will be yours.

Is there space in your life
for your beloved to blossom?
Is your physical environment cluttered with
stuff?
Is your body contaminated with tensions and
toxins?
Is your mind full of noise?
Empty yourself.
Make space.

12

BEHIND THE MASKS

Seeking to appear important creates blindness.
Polishing your image is a waste of time.
Do you want to spend your lives
as two masks,
forever hiding from each other?

Seeking to sound impressive creates deafness.
Let your words be simple, direct
and filled with love.

Seeking to please everyone creates tastelessness.
State your desires honestly.
Listen with acceptance.
Forgive graciously.

☯

The energy needed
to maintain an image of yourself
while molding another one for your beloved
would light a small city.
Let go and discover your hearts and souls
behind the masks.

13

No Need to Strive

Relationship bliss does not sit on a mountain top
waiting for you to climb up to it.
It sits on your shoulder
waiting for you to notice it.

Joy does not reside in some future world.
It sits across the table from you,
needing only your undivided attention.

Pleasure does not hide in your fantasies
It is ready to come alive
at the next touch of skin to skin.

☯

Are you together right now?
Stop reading.
Stop whatever you are doing.
Put on a piece of music that pleases you.
Come to each other's arms
and dance for five minutes.
Then return to your activities.
What are you waiting for?

14

RETURN TO YOUR CENTER

If you make a show of your love,
it will hide itself.
If you babble on about it,
your words will fail.
If you grasp and cling to it,
it will slip through your fingers.

You cannot approach that which has no
        beginning.
You cannot lose that which has no end.
You do not have to protect it.
How then can you experience it?
As a swimmer experiences the water.
Dive in.

☯

If you are feeling somewhat separate
and distant from your beloved,
do the things that stabilize you.
Walk, dance, paint, meditate,
write, build, play, or sing.
When you return to your center
you will find your beloved waiting.

15

WITHIN YOU

Within you is a place of love and grace.
It is a place without fear
where there is no need to defend or prove,
no need to lie or hide.
From this place spring words of truth,
actions of courage,
and a life of love.
Wait patiently for the voices of fear in your
        mind
to cease their frantic call to action.
Become aware of what the next clear step
of love might be.

Be patient with yourself.
The qualities of a lover
do not depend on externals.
They take root in your own soul
and grow as you attend to them.
They all lie within you.

16

CONFIDENCE

Your relationship begins with the Tao
and returns to the Tao.
Therefore you may watch it unfold
with confidence.
Beginning and ending,
searching and finding,
living and dying,
are all part of the Tao.
If you look deeply you will discover
that loss is not the final word.

Fear often appears either
as a lashing out
or as withdrawal.
The next time you do either of these
think,
"What am I afraid of?"
This is the real issue.
When this issue is shared,
confidence returns.

17

WITH FREEDOM
AND WITH JOY

If your beloved becomes dependent on you
resentment will follow.
If your beloved is in awe of you
it may feel good
but is very dangerous.
If your beloved sings your praises far and wide
it seems wonderful,
but disappointment lurks just around the corner.

Best of all is for your beloved to respond to you
with freedom and with joy,
to grow in confidence and strength,
and to become capable of great
        accomplishments.
You allow this to occur by your gifts
of trust, assurance, and freedom.

Of course we enjoy each other's praise.
It can be part of a healthy joyous relationship.
But be careful of behaving in ways
that are calculated to generate
praise or dependence.
You are not each other's audience
for the playing out of ego dreams.
You are each other's beloved.

18

It Can't Be Forced

When the soul of a relationship is lost
self-help books appear on the coffee table.
When grace is not experienced
behavior is scrutinized carefully.
When harmony is missing
the talk is about, "my needs," and "your needs."
When the relationship is dying
loyalty and fidelity are demanded.

Return to your heart.
Here is where your relationship must live.

☯

"Working on a relationship"
can be an illusion.
Trying to carve your relationship
into an idealized image
will damage you both.
The real thing lives
within each of you.
It can't be forced,
only allowed to emerge.
Can you see it?

19

HAPPINESS IS AS
NATURAL AS BREATHING

Do you believe that nagging each other
will bring happiness to your relationship?
Eliminate the pressure to change
and you both will find true joy.
Eliminate demands for loyalty and commitment
and true faithfulness will spring into being.

Happiness and contentment
blossom naturally in the heart that is open.
But the heart that is criticized and pressured
will close
and only the weeds of resentment
and bitterness will grow.

The bad news is that
 you cannot make each other happy.
The good news is that
happiness is as natural as breathing.
Trust its presence in your hearts
and give it room to grow.

20

A PRIVATE MATTER

Why be anxious about what others think
concerning the two of you?
Are you building your relationship
on public opinion polls?

Others build their relationships
on the basis of looking good.
The power of your love is hidden from view.
It is not for display.

Others search for ways
to make their relationships exciting.
Yours appears dull to them.
They cannot see deeply enough.

Others strive to accumulate
the trappings of success.
You and your beloved seem unambitious,
settling for simplicity.
Your love comes from a source
others cannot see.

☯

Do not judge your relationship
on the basis of image.
The deepest soul relationships
are very private matters.
Honor the privacy of yours.

21

ILLUMINATION

There is a light that fills the cosmos.
It is the unified field of energy that
some call God,
some call Mystery,
some call the Tao,
and some give no name at all.
It doesn't matter what you call the light.
But realize that it manifests
in a special manner
in your relationship.
It illuminates your life together
and cannot be hidden
or extinguished.

☯

Sit in silence and look attentively
at each other this evening.
Do you see the light?
Look carefully.

22

RELATIONSHIP PARADOXES

Paradoxes abound in love
and they must be fully lived.
Being wounded is the only way to healing.
Being at fault is the only path to forgiveness.
Feeling empty allows for satisfaction.
Longing for another brings passion's fulfillment.

Paradoxes cannot be solved
as problems are solved.
They can only be accepted
and cherished.
Are the current issues in your relationship
problems,
or paradoxes?

23

LIVE YOUR EMOTIONS FULLY

Live your moods fully and appropriately
and your beloved will receive the gift
of who you truly are.
Let your anger be honest, brief, and
  compassionate,
not fueled by lingering resentment.
Let your joy be rich and hearty,
filled with laughter and dance.
Let your grief be open and full
and your tears will be a cleansing rain.
This is the natural way of things.

By acknowledging and revealing your feelings
in honest non-hurtful ways,
you give a gift of wholeness
to both you and your beloved.
Are you restricting your relationship
by repressing either joy or sorrow?
Is hidden anger turning to resentment?
Who are you trying to fool?

24

PUSHING DOES NOT BRING MATURITY

If you are always pushing yourself
your love will not come to maturity.
Pushing implies a preconceived direction
while maturity considers many directions.
Striving for great achievement narrows focus,
while maturity opens to many options.
Devotion to your career brings power and
    reputation,
while maturity brings devotion to each other.

☯

Work a modest number of hours,
then go home.
At home there is no need for pushing,
no need for striving.
Here at home your love finds its full expression.

25

THE TAO OF LOVE

Before the universe was born
the solitary, infinite, changeless, formless,
        eternal Tao
was.
This Tao gave birth to the universe
and also to the love
that flows in your relationship.
This flowing love binds you and your beloved
to all things in creation
and returns you again to the Tao,
no beginning
no end.

The wonder of your life together
is not due to your effort.
It is a natural unfolding of the Tao.
You can trust it.
You can rest on it.
You are not generating it
by the power of your will.
Let yourself enjoy this day,
watching the various threads
add their contribution to the tapestry of your
     life.

26

FAITHFULNESS

Restlessness causes the mind to wander.
You pace the floor wondering what next to do
to bring the passion back to your life.
You try this and that
but nothing satisfies.
Then the thought emerges,
"Perhaps a different person . . ."

Instead be still
and calm your fears.
Let the restlessness run its course
and fade.
When it passes, your beloved
will still be there
and your love will flame anew.

Faithfulness in a relationship
is not so much a product of willpower,
as of patience.
Patiently let the storms of your mind
blow past without uprooting you.
Your thoughts will always return to your
beloved.

27

WHEN YOU HEAR THE
URGINGS OF YOUR HEART

The path of love
is illumined by intuition.
Intuition connects the mind
to the heart,
and creates openness and flexibility.

Do not hold on to preferences
that things or people
be one way or another.
This will muffle intuition's voice.
Instead be ready to change course
at a moment's notice
when you hear the urgings of your heart.

Sadly, we all learn the power of our intuition
by experiencing the consequences
of ignoring it.
I ignored mine for many years
and paid a heavy price.
But, when it truly counted,
I followed it to my own heart's mate.

28

ALWAYS RETURN

It is good to know your strength
but always return to your flexibility.
If you can cradle your beloved in your arms
in nurturing gentleness,
love will flow through you.

It is good to achieve things
but always return to anonymity.
Your beloved does not need your achievements
but needs your uncomplicated soul.

It is good to work for change,
but always return to what is.
If you accept all things whether painful or
     joyful,
you will always know
that you belong to each other
and to the Tao.

☯

Return today,
to that which brings you life:
enfolding, caressing,
soothing, nurturing,
forgiving and accepting.

29

A Time for Every Mood

Let your moods come and go.
Each of you will feel sad and happy;
full of vigor and exhausted;
peaceful and anxious;
loving and withdrawn;
and each of these feelings
will insist on having its proper time.
If you cease trying to control them,
you will create for each other
a smoother, happier way.
They will arise and fall
against a backdrop of contentment and serenity.

☯

The yin and yang of life
are obvious in our changing moods.
The less you worry about them
the freer they will be to play their proper role,
and the freer you each will be
to live in joy.

30

WIN OR LOSE?

Your relationship will always
have issues to face.
If you try to win your own way
you will lose.
If you attempt to dominate
by the force of your clever arguments,
the brilliance of your personality,
or the righteousness of your cause,
you will reap a whirlwind of trouble.

If you win,
your beloved loses.
If your beloved wins,
you lose.
Is this the path of love?

No solution ever emerges from love
that creates a winner and a loser.
Ever!
Love always finds a way,
with patience, effort, and compassion,
to meet the needs of both.
Have patience.
Keep looking.

31

DISCOVERY, OR DEFENSE?

Will the time ever come
when you must defend your views
or your feelings?
Could your beloved's own pain
ever cause an attack?
Be careful.
What manifests as an attack on you
is really a statement of fear.
If you attack in return
the fear escalates.

Defend yourself when necessary
with gentle confidence,
never with glee or satisfaction.
For when the battle is over
and you survey the damage done,
it will be a time for mourning.

Books on "fighting fair"
give me pause.
Rather than finding better ways to fight,
might you be able to find
the roots of your conflicts?
This is certainly a difficult task,
filled with emotion and fear.
But if your goal is discovery
instead of defense,
deep peace is just ahead.

32

FACE YOUR FEARS

Your relationship is not
just one more arrangement
designed to keep you
from facing your fears.
It is the safe and stable ground
upon which you can stand
to face whatever comes.
Do not use your beloved
to hide from yourself.

Shortly after our last move
I developed a massive case of poison oak.
In my misery I became vulnerable
to old feelings of shame and regret.
For several evenings my beloved Nancy sat with
me,
as I talked, cried, ranted and raved,
safe enough at last
to be afraid.

33

TRUE NEEDS

Knowing each other well
is considered important.
But love begins with knowing yourself
and what you truly need.

When your beloved meets your needs
you may consider it a blessing.
But true blessing begins
when needs are simple and few.
Touching fingers and holding hands,
tasting wine and hearing music,
making love and sharing deeply,
then sleeping soundly through the night.
Let these become your true needs.

The first time my beloved and I held hands
we were walking across a grassy park.
We were shy and cautious
and the only intimacy we shared that day
was the intertwining of our fingers.
It was enough.

34

THE WAY YOU
TREAT EACH OTHER

The love you give each other
can be your greatest service.
Like ripples in a pond
your love spreads out in circles
and changes all it touches.
The way you treat each other
becomes the way you treat all things.

I have met many people
who love their important causes
but treat those closest to them
with contempt.
If you wish to live lives of service
learn to cherish each other fully.
This will lead not to self-absorption
but to greater compassion for all.

35

THE GIFT OF SELF

Let your only ambition be to let
your beloved see you clearly,
your fears, your hopes,
your scars, your dreams,
your joy, your sorrow,
your desires, your passions
and your innermost life.
This is giving the gift of self.
If you do not give this gift,
what is the use of giving any other?

◑

What is more important,
finding each day a bit more truth
about each other;
or striving another day
to maintain an illusion?
How are you spending this day?

36

ROOM TO BREATHE

If there are issues between you,
they must have room to breathe.
If you repress or ignore them,
they will smolder on.
If they are exposed to the air
they may flare up for a moment
but will die for lack of fuel.

☯

Don't be afraid of discussing problems,
or expressing fears.
Just do it tenderly and without judgment.
This gives each of you the chance
to accept, to nurture, and to trust.

37

NATURAL DESIRES

Relationships can be distorted
by the artificial creation of desire
by those who use words
on behalf of sellers of goods.
These artificially created desires
can never be adequately satisfied
because they are not natural.
Natural desires have their fulfillment
contained within them
for they emerge from the Tao
and are satisfied by the Tao.

It may be helpful to talk some evening
about what you truly want.
Happiness?—How will you know?
Success?—How do you measure it?
Possessions?—What and why?
How is your relationship affected
by each of these desires?
Which emerge from your center
and which are imposed from without?
Consider carefully.

38

WILL POWER

If the heart of your relationship is lost,
you will try to hang on by willpower.
Willpower will fail and be replaced
by the appearance of good behavior.
Keeping up appearances
is the beginning of the end.
The energy of your love
must arise from deeper sources.

Force of will can be a virtue.
It can carry you through some dry and barren
    times.
But it cannot substitute for the deeper springs
of energy, passion and joy
that first brought you together.
Keep these springs alive!
Know how to find your way back to them
when you wander away.
Drink always from them.

39

A SHINING JEWEL

The wonders of the Tao—-
the nighttime sky,
the dancing waters,
the forests full of life,
need no improvement.

Your beloved's life is precious,
a natural wonder,
a shining jewel.
Don't tamper with it.
It does not need polishing,
improving,
or correcting.

Neither do you.

Don't bring yourselves the misery
of, "If only he'd . . ."
or, "She needs to . . ."
or, "Why don't I . . ."
Delight in what you are right now
and you will both have room to become
everything that you can be.

40

HERE IS WHERE
YOUR LOVE WAS BORN

Let your shoulders drop and your eyes close.
Soften your muscles and remember a child's
    flexibility.
Breathe deeply and let your busy thoughts fade
    away.
There is a place of stillness and quiet
underneath your thoughts.
Here is where your love was born.

Some call it meditation.
Some call it relaxation.
Some call it prayer.
Whatever you call it,
do it.
It is the center
from which the rest of your life emerges.
Without it
your relationship is a carefully acted play.

41

A DIFFERENT SLANT

One couple finds the Tao absurd,
so absurd that they laugh out loud.
They have no interest in mysterious things.

Another couple finds the Tao appealing,
but terribly impractical.
They have learned to live another way
and cannot see to change.

Yet another couple hears of the Tao
and immediately begins to live by it.
Their hearts are truly one.

The Tao may seem unrealistic
but contains deep truth;
may look difficult but is very simple;
may feel childish but embodies wisdom;
may sound indifferent but harbors great
        compassion.
Look carefully.

The Tao gives a slightly different slant
on the truths of your relationship.
No rules or easy steps.
Just a look into the heart of things.
Create your own steps to live it out.

42

TWO ENERGIES OF LOVE

Two energies always play
whenever you make love.
The active Yang dances
with the receptive Yin.
One of you leads the way,
beckoning the other to follow.
One gives pleasure,
the other receives.
Then Yin and Yang change places.
Giving and receiving flow together,
over, under, around, and through.
Yin and Yang together
make the ecstasy of love.

Sexual pleasure has many moods and forms,
but it is always a dance.
Who plays the role of leader
and who of follower,
changes from encounter to encounter
and moment to moment.
But remember it is a dance,
not a contest or a performance.

43

YIELDING MAINTAINS
A BALANCE

Be gentle and tender with one another
without being passive.
Passivity leads to resentment
while gentleness gives birth to understanding.
Yield to each other
without surrendering.
Surrendering means the loss of self hood
while yielding maintains the balance
of self and other.

Martial artists know this truth.
A soft flexible body survives
the hardest of attacks
with balance and poise.
A rigid body is easily broken.
Look to your gentleness,
practice your flexibility.
At the same time maintain
your balance and your self hood.

44

CONVERSATION

Do not talk of fame and reputation,
either of yourselves or others.
Such conversations are illusions
and do not contribute to your joy and peace.
Your conversations help create your world.
Speak of delight, not dissatisfaction.
Speak of hope, not despair.
Let your words bind up wounds,
not cause them.

☯

Conversation is one of the central arts of love.
It requires attention, effort and skill.
It demands open minds and compassionate
          hearts.
How many of your conversations
reflect discontentment with life as it is,
or with each other as you are?
Can you begin to turn them
to expressions of delight and hope,
of encouragement, learning and healing?

45

PERFECTION

Perfection cannot be attained,
but it can be noticed.
If you pay full attention
to what seems flawed and ordinary
you will notice the perfection
hiding beneath appearances.
If you pay full attention to each other
you will notice how perfectly
you are each becoming who you really are.
By seeing the perfection in what is
you allow the creation
of what is not.

What is, is.
Each of you are what you are.
That's the way it is.
If you can learn to take delight
in what seems flawed and wrong in each other,
you create the atmosphere that enables
growth and change.
Sounds impossible?
Try it.

46

OF WHAT ARE YOU AFRAID?

All that is negative
and injurious to your relationship
is born of fear.
Fear births jealousy,
fuels anger,
and prompts harsh words.
The most difficult times
contain the greatest fear.
If you would live in love,
do not be afraid.

My spouse and I are furthest apart
when we are the most afraid.
But when the fears are spoken and faced,
our intimacy is not only restored
but deepened.
Ask yourselves the question,
"Of what are we afraid?"
Honest answers, mindfully spoken
and courageously heard,
will set you free.

47

A SACRED SPACE

Your love requires space in which to grow.
This space must be safe enough
to allow your hearts to be revealed.
It must offer refreshment for your spirits
and renewal for your minds.
It must be a space made sacred
by the quality of your honesty,
attention, love, and compassion.
It may be anywhere,
inside or out,
but it must exist.

My spouse and I have a small altar
in the corner of our bedroom.
A budding branch, some candles, water, earth
and other tokens of our lives rest there.
Before it we have talked, meditated,
laughed and cried.
In this space we have danced
and joined in sacred passion.
Where is your space?

48

SUBTRACTION CAN ADD

In pursuit of the perfect relationship
people add each day more and more things to
     their lives,
hoping that one day they will have what they
     need.
But in your love you have discovered
that less and less is needed.
You subtract daily from the things that distract.
One day you discover that you have always had
everything you ever needed.

The question, "What do I need
in order to be happy?" is difficult to answer.
Careers are good, children are a gift,
money is useful, health is a blessing,
but what is essential?
Talk with each other about it.
Perhaps less than you think.

49

GENUINE AFFECTION

When your beloved delights you
you respond with affection—
a smile, a hug, a touch of the hand
gently on bare skin.
But when your beloved disappoints you,
can you still respond with affection?
Can you still open your arms, hold tenderly,
caress healingly, and talk lovingly?
This affection is genuine.
It does not depend
on the behavior of others.
It lies within you at all times.

Can you see each other at your very worst
and respond in love to what you see?
Can you see the lost and lonely child,
hiding behind the unpleasant behavior?
Can you hear the pleas for tenderness?

50

DO NOT
WITHHOLD YOURSELF

Do not withhold yourselves from each other.
To withhold is to lie to yourself
and to each other.
Do not withhold your feelings
but share them openly and with compassion.
Do not withhold your forgiveness
but give it freely as a natural gift.
Do not withhold your delight
but dance and laugh and play with ease.
Do not withhold your body,
but give it often in the myriad ways of passion.

Withholding comes from fear of loss.
We hesitate and resist,
trying to insulate ourselves from pain.
Don't be afraid.
Look for ways to open up
and trust each other a bit more fully.
Feel how it eases the tension
in your body and in your mind.

51

DEMANDING NOTHING, SUPPLYING EVERYTHING

The Tao demands nothing of your love,
yet it acts in every kiss,
every touch,
and every embrace.
It suffers every insult,
bleeds in every wound,
and flows in every tear
yet never takes offense.
You can always trust it
for it has nothing to prove.
It needs nothing
yet supplies everything.

The acceptance and generosity of the Tao
is difficult to understand and to accept.
Not possessive, demanding, judging or pushing.
Yet full of creativity and power.
Remember that this is your own nature.
It is what you are really like
underneath the scars and behind the masks.
Become yourself and you will become like the
Tao.

52

LOOK TO THE BEGINNING

If you trace problems in your relationship
back to the beginning
you will find their seeds
were sown and then ignored.
They grew unnoticed until their fruit
ripened and surprised you.
But if you can find
where the seeds were sown,
there you will find the roots as well.
And if you remove the roots
your problems will wither.

The real issues are seldom what they appear to
        be.
Look deeply into your conflicts.
What little seed,
planted long ago,
is coming into bloom?
When you find the origins
do not recriminate each other
or worry about who sowed the seed.
Pull out the roots.

53

EFFORTLESS

Your love together grows
with effortlessness and simplicity.
You will know when you are trying too hard.
There will be an increase in activity
and a decrease in thoughtfulness.
There will be an increase in effort
and a decrease in peace.
There will be an increase in buying things
and a decrease in the enjoyment of them.
There will be an increase in talking
and a decrease in listening.

Living effortlessly is not easy.
It requires great attention
to the simple nurturing activities
that we would rather avoid.
It requires listening and holding.
It requires much time spent in reading love
poems
and taking leisurely walks by moonlight.
It requires devoting whole days to the art of
love.
When you begin doing these things
you will see how effortless they become.

54

TRANSFORMING POWER

Your love contains the power
of a thousand suns.
It unfolds as naturally and effortlessly
as does a flower,
and graces the world with its blooming.
Its beauty radiates a transforming energy
that enlivens all who see it.
Because of you, compassion and joy
are added to the world.
That is why the stars sing together
because of your love.

❧

The world will never know love, respect,
kindness and tolerance
until you experience them
in the safety of your love.
When you do,
it will.

55

FOREVER YOUNG

If you accept each other exactly as you are,
you will not be disappointed
and your souls will remain young and fresh
If you don't set your hearts on any one result,
you will not be frustrated by events
and your love will remain strong and vital.
If you welcome events as they come
you will not be anxious about the future
and your relationship will remain supple and
     alive.

☯

You have seen couples
for whom despair and frustration
have become a way of life.
They sleep-walk through their days
blaming, complaining, and dying.
You have also seen those
whose aging life together
has brought softness, gentleness and wisdom.
Which are the two of you becoming?

56

WITHOUT TALKING

Those who live continually in love,
seldom talk about it.
It exists outside your
words,
thoughts,
feelings,
and senses.
Yet fills up all that you are.
Too much talking hinders
your ability to hear it.

Spend a whole day with your beloved
without talking.
Do not read, listen to radio or watch television.
Just be with each other and notice how you feel,
even when it seems strange.
Discover who you are
without all of these things.
Express your essence to each other
wordlessly.

57

FORGET RULES

If you create "rules for our relationship"
you will blame each other for breaking them.
If you develop lofty goals and plans,
you will always struggle to achieve them.
If you strive continually for perfection,
you will always be dissatisfied.

Forget rules
and you will naturally do
what is best for your beloved.
Forget goals and plans
and your life together will thrive.
Forget perfection
and you will be perfect.

Goals, plans and efforts
are not necessarily bad.
But remember that you already
have everything you need.
Let a touch, a kiss, and an embrace
be your reminders.

58

ACCEPT THINGS AS THEY ARE

You cannot force each other
to be or feel a certain way.
If you insist on happiness
you create misery.
If you insist on achievement
you create failure.
If you insist on a certain behavior
you insure its opposite.

But your complete acceptance
creates serenity and comfort,
and your straightforwardness
creates security and honesty.

Give each other the freedom
to experience and to feel whatever comes.
If your beloved is sad, or angry, or afraid
don't be threatened by those feelings.
Let them just be there,
part of the reality of the moment.
If your beloved errs or fails, accept these things
        as well.
In every mood or circumstance
let your love be tender and constant.

59

LOVE IS THE
BASIC ENERGY OF LIFE

Love is the basic energy of life.
Nothing can stop your love from growing
because everything is fuel for its fire.
Like a tree that bends easily in the wind,
it accommodates to the natural events of life
and does not become overwhelmed.
It uses the times we call good
to fashion dances of joy.
It uses the times we call bad
to create the depths of our compassion.
Nothing is wasted.
Nothing is lost.

☯

When you promise each other
to be there "in sickness and in health"
you cooperate with the energy of love
which uses all circumstances
for its own good purposes.
Don't be discouraged by trials you now face.
Burn them in the furnace of your heart
and turn them into life's own energy.

60

KEEP YOUR PERSPECTIVE

Nurturing your love
is like tending a small garden.
If you keep pulling up the plants
to see if the roots are growing
you will harvest nothing.

If you focus on your troubles
you give them added power.
Step aside as would a martial arts master.
The troubles still exist,
but you are not unbalanced by their blows.
They lose their power to disturb.
They become food for growth.

Scrutinizing every detail of your relationship
searching for hidden motives and meanings
will drive you both crazy.
Remember the many things that bring balance
to your life together:
the touches, caresses, smiles and kindnesses.
Take walks.
Share simple intimate meals.
And wash each other's hair
in the bath by candlelight.
These will keep your perspective clear.

61

YOUR LIFE TOGETHER
IS UNLIKE ALL OTHERS

Comparing your relationship
to other relationships
will lead you far afield.
You will either inflate yourselves,
"Thank goodness we don't behave like the
      Taylors!"
Or you will diminish yourselves,
"If only we were as romantic as the Wilsons."
Instead of looking at others,
look honestly at yourselves.
You life together is unlike all others.
It must become uniquely itself.

☯

Your relationship becomes itself
by considering the questions,
"What do we truly like to do?
How do we really feel about that?
What actually brings us peace and joy?"
Forget for a moment what others say.
Forget what couples are supposed to do.
If there were no "supposed to's"
what would you do?

62

YOU ARE BOUND TOGETHER
BY STRANDS OF SOUL

What draws you together
and keeps your passion alive?
Not your economic needs.
Not your fear of loneliness.
Not your habits.
These may bind lives together
but they are not the bindings of your love.

You are bound together by strands of soul,
spun from the deepest regions of your hearts.
Invisible to the casual eye,
these are the ties that bind you.

☯

There are surely habits and mutual needs
that are part of your life together.
But remember the deeper reasons,
the intangible mysteries,
the seeming magic of your love.
Weave the fabric of your life
with these threads.

63

EMBRACE YOUR DIFFICULTIES

Embrace your difficulties
as they arise in your relationship.
You belong to the Tao and to each other
and therefore need not fear problems.
Since you are not afraid,
you welcome the problems
while they are still small.
Since they are small,
they resolve themselves.

If you are annoyed
or bothered by something.
Don't be afraid to face it honestly.
You may see that it is trivial
and dismiss it without mention.
Or you may need to bring it up
in the safety of your love.
Either way it becomes a tool
of growth and maturity
instead of a stumbling stone.

64

THE SMALL STEP

If you are attentive and careful,
you can notice the tiny seeds of kindness
and give them nourishment.
You can see hints of discord
and easily turn them to peace.
If you are blindly pursuing your agendas
you ignore these seeds and hints,
and reap a harvest of trouble.

Seeds of love can be fed and watered,
but never forced to grow.
You do not have to teach a seed its duty,
it grows because that is its nature.
You do not have to teach each other love.
It will flourish because that is your nature.
But you must be patient.

Be patient as the seeds of your love
grow and mature.
It does not have to happen all at once.
Each day, each moment,
adds one more small element
to the magnificent pattern.

65

No Others Love Exactly
as Do the Two of You

Be wary of relationship gurus.
They impose their own thoughts
and their own experience upon their words
and teach you what they know.
But this may not be
what you need to know yourself.
No others love exactly
as do the two of you.

☯

We are all too quick to turn to "experts"
instead of turning to ourselves.
We end up trying to construct our relationships
in line with the models they prescribe.
Listen and read with an open mind,
but let your own experience of each other
be your final guide.

66

A FIELD OF DREAMS

You do not exist to fulfill each other's dreams,
but to show each other the place
where these hopes are born.
Do not impose your dreams upon each other.
You must each follow the images
that arise within your own hearts.
But you can create for each other an open field
where dreams can grow and flourish.

☯

Do not try to "tweak" or modify
the dreams of your beloved.
These are deeply personal
and must be treated with great respect.
Giving help and encouragement to each other
in the following of dreams
is good and proper.
But the dreams themselves are sacred
and must be given great respect.

67

RETURN TO THESE THINGS

In the confusion of a complex world,
clarity of purpose can be lost.
In the bustle of a hurried life,
patience is forgotten.
In the midst of a multitude of distractions,
passion can fade away.

Slow down and think clearly.
Your passion thrives on simple things.
Return to these things.

This week:
Instead of the morning news,
a walk together hand-in-hand;
Instead of a power lunch,
some warm bread, cheese,
and the love poetry of Rumi;
Instead of *The Tonight Show*,
tender love by candlelight.

68

PLAY WITH EACH OTHER AS DO CHILDREN

Play with each other as do children.
Laugh and sing and skip.
Tumble in each other's arms
and squeal with delight.
Play games without a thought
of winning or losing.
Play with words
and make each other laugh.
Play with each other's bodies
and make each other sigh.
It is your playfulness
that makes you like the Tao.

Our culture has filled play
with effort, expense, and intensity.
Simplify your play.
You don't need expensive toys.
You don't need advanced technology.
You don't need athletic skill.
You only need each other.

69

THE HEALING PURPOSE
OF CONFLICT

If you must oppose one another,
do it as a physician
nursing a body back to health,
never as an attacking general,
leading an army to victory.
To attack is to believe that your beloved
is the enemy you must conquer.
Your beloved is never the enemy.
Let your conflict be a source of revelation.
Learn the deeper, subtler, hidden aspects of each
     other.
This will be the victory
each of you is seeking.

Disagreement is natural,
conflict is part of human life.
But your relationship is not a war.
You do not have to win.
What you have to do is learn,
about your beloved,
and about yourself.
This is the primary purpose of conflict.

70

You Must Be Able to Taste Your Love

Working out the details
of daily life together
is a proper function of the mind.
But your real experience of each other
is a product of your senses.
It is as tangible as a kiss.
You must be able to taste your love
as you would taste a ripe strawberry.

Touch more—gentle touches, passionate
    touches,
 and comforting touches.
Kiss more—soft kisses, demanding kisses, and
    healing kisses.
Hear more—sounds of books read aloud, sounds
    of heartbeats,
and sounds of sharing.
See more—sparkle of eyes, texture of skin, and
    subtle movements.
Smell more—aromas of meals, fragrance of
    flowers,
and the familiar scent of each other's skin.

71

KNOWING HOW TO DANCE

Each coming together is a new dance
with a lover who knows how to lead
and how to follow.
The moods and events of life
are always changing.
Confidence in each other does not come
from the ability to predict each other's routine,
but from knowing how to dance
to whatever music plays.

☯

Dancing is a wonderful metaphor
for a life of love together.
Shifting your pace from fast to slow,
from free-form to patterned,
from joyous to melancholy,
is the secret of success.
Sometimes you will dance alone
to different rhythms,
but never too far away.

72

THE RELIGION OF
YOUR HEART

Be cautious of religion.
Rules and doctrines are lifeless things,
dried leaves blowing in the Autumn breeze.
The Mystery of the Tao cannot be taught,
it can only be revered and trusted.
Stand beside each other hand in hand
and watch the moon together.
Hold each other close
and be completely present in your passion.
Walk beside the splashing stream
and let your thoughts float on the water.
You will see and know.

☯

Spirituality touches the deepest feelings of the
　　heart.
Do not seek to convert or enlighten one
　　another.
Seek only to understand and cherish
the uniqueness of each other's soul.
Treating each other with acceptance and grace
is the religion of your heart.

73

SPRING OF LOVE

The presence of the Tao
living in your relationship is certain.
You do not need to understand it.
It will not impose itself upon you.
It will not work according to your plan.
Yet it will never fail to accomplish its purpose.
It is within you like a spring
of unconditional love.
It will quench your fears
and nourish your life together.

When your life together seems dry and dusty,
imagine yourself a well-digger.
Not far beneath the surface
is the water that will refresh and renew.
Imagine how it will feel when you find it.
Dig for it.
Trust that it will be there.

74

THE TAO CONTAINS ALL
LOSS AND GAIN

Events are always changing
and nothing can be grasped.
Change always means losing something
and gaining something else.
There is no loss without a gain,
no gain without a loss.
Therefore do not cling to anything;
to a possession, a circumstance, or a person.
Do not even cling to life.
Death itself must lead to gain
for life and death are both within the Tao.

Committing your life to another person
is a great change,
filled with both loss and gain.
You lose some independence
You gain a world of love.
Gaining a world of love,
you fear its loss.
But you need not be afraid.
The Tao contains all loss and gain
and contains each of you as well.

75

WHY ELSE ARE YOU
TOGETHER?

When expectations become numerous,
pressure grows within a relationship.
When pressure grows
it becomes explosive.
You did not come together to be molded
by each other's expectations.
You are together to celebrate and enjoy
the absolute wonder of each other,
to warm your nights and brighten your days,
and to delight in each other's differences.

Pressure can be applied in many ways—
stony silence and withdrawal until the other
        apologizes,
criticism until they learn,
withholding or giving sexual pleasure
depending on their behavior.
This is no way to live.
Let go of expectations, release the pressure,
and enjoy each other.
Why else are you together?

76

THE COSMOS STILL WAITS IN THOSE EYES

In your early days together
your souls and bodies opened to each other.
You moved with grace and ease
and your days and nights were filled
with new and wondrous thoughts.

If you remain delighted with each new moment
and open to surprises,
you are on the path of life.
If you have become rigid and bored,
complaining and criticizing when faced with
    change,
you are on the path of death.

There was a time when dreams and plans took
      wings.
Your beloved's eyes contained the cosmos,
inviting you to travel to distant worlds.
Why have you narrowed your vision?
Circumstances have changed
and life has dealt you blows.
But the cosmos still waits in those eyes.
Look carefully.

77

BRING BALANCE

Let your souls unite as your bodies blend
in the intimacy of love,
but also let your spirits walk
in solitude and silence.
Balance in a relationship is not static,
like a counterbalanced scale.
It is dynamic like a spinning gyroscope,
or a leaping twirling dance.
Yin and yang,
you and me,
give and take,
together and alone
are each part of the Tao.

Opposite energies each have their place.
Too much attention can be smothering.
Too little may feel like abandonment.
Is it time for physical passion,
or gentle conversation?
Time to be together, or to be alone?
You must learn to sense these rhythms
and allow them to have their time.
Which is needed at this moment in your life?

78

AS A RIVER MAKES LOVE
TO THE EARTH

Make love to each other
as a river makes love to the earth—
soft and yielding, yet powerful and overcoming.
Surround the rigid places with softness,
and wash them away.
Flow into the open places
with power and strength,
bringing relief from drought.
In this manner your love making will bring
joy and healing to all of life.

Sexual love is not an athletic performance.
It is the supreme form of yin and yang,
active and receptive energies,
dancing to their eternal music.
Let your love express a wide array of moods.
Let it be passionate and ecstatic.
Let it be long and leisurely.
Let it be brief and intense.
Let it be funny and playful.
Let it be romantic.
Let it be pure pleasure.
Let it be healing and comforting.

79

WELCOME YOUR OWN AND
EACH OTHER'S FAILURES

Welcome your own
and each other's failures.
They enable you to
correct your illusions,
refine your spirits,
and model your love.
In this wonderful situation
there is never need for blame.

There is a saying in Japanese business,
"Fix the problem, not the blame."
There will be times when your beloved
will truly disappoint you
and you will be greatly tempted
to assign guilt and blame.
If instead you work together
with creativity and imagination,
and together solve the problem,
your love will be unbounded.

80

IT IS VERY GOOD

Your life together produces
great blessing and contentment.
You are busy enough with work to be satisfied
but have ample time to play.
Your financial needs are modest
for you need very little to be very happy.
Your spirits are fed
by the quiet and solitude you allow each other.
Your bodies merge in the pleasures of love.
You share food and song,
work and play,
sorrow and joy,
all without fear.
And when you come to die you think,
"It was good, is good, and will always be good."

Contentment in your relationship
is not a naive expectation.
The ups and downs of life
and the swing of changing moods
do not have to destroy you.
Can you see the happiness
that lies within your reach?

81

You Do Not Need Words
to Prove Your Love

You do not need words
to prove your love.
The proof lies in simple actions.
Listening with attention,
seeing with acceptance,
touching with tenderness,
this is the way of the Tao.

☯

I know the great mystery of love
and the overarching Tao
can be trusted.
I know this not because of any words.
I know it because I touched it
when I first touched Nancy's hand.
No matter what happens,
trust the power of your love.
All will be well.

WILLIAM MARTIN, husband and father of two grown children, has been a student of the Tao for 10 years. A graduate of the University of California, Berkeley, and Western Theological Seminary, he has worked as a research scientist for the Department of the Navy, a clergyman, and a college instructor in counseling, communications, and the humanities. Today, he and his wife Nancy operate The Still Point, an educational and consulting center. He conducts workshops and seminars on subjects including tai chi chuan, Zen, stages of spiritual development, mediation, and religious burnout. He and his wife live in Chico, California. He can be reached by e-mail at Stlpnt@aol.com.

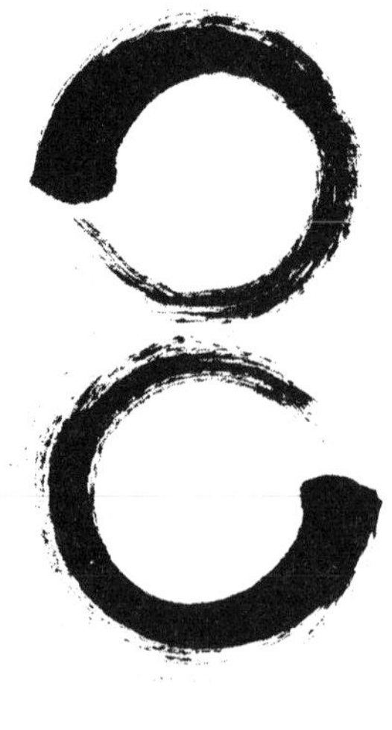